My First English/Spanish
Dictionary
of Sentences

Armelle Modéré

BARRON'S

Contents

School is over, Dorie is happy to be **home**.

Las clases se han acabado, Dorie está contenta de estar en **casa**.

House
La casa

Dad is sitting on the sofa in the **living room**. He is reading.

Papá está sentado en el sofá del **salón**. Está leyendo.

Dorie loves taking care of the **garden**.

A Dorie le encanta cuidar el **jardín**.

Dorie plays
on the **bed**.
Dorie juega en
la **cama**.

She often draws sitting
at her **desk**.
A menudo dibuja sentada
en su **escritorio**.

Dad is going to put the car
in the **garage**.
Papá va a poner el carro
en el **garaje**.

Family
La familia

Good morning! My name is Tom and this is my **little sister**, Emily.

¡Buenos días! Me llamo Tom y esta es mi **hermanita**, Emily.

These are my **parents**, Amy and Peter.

Estos son mis **padres**, Amy y Peter.

Swiffy and Lily are also part of the **family**.

Swiffy y Lily también forman parte de la **familia**.

Tom loves playing with his **cousins**.
A Tom le gusta mucho jugar con sus **primos**.

Tom's **aunt** has just had a baby.
La **tía** de Tom acaba de tener un bebé.

Grandpa and **Grandma** have come to see us today.
El **abuelito** y la **abuelita** han venido a vernos hoy.

The **alarm clock** is ringing. Time to get up!
Ha sonado el **despertador**.
¡Es hora de levantarse!

Time to get up
Hora de levantarse

Mom gives Ted a big **hug**. Did you sleep well?
Mamá da un gran **abrazo** a Ted. ¿Has dormido bien?

Dad is up already.
He is **having breakfast**.
Papá ya está levantado.
Está **desayunando**.

When Ted finishes his breakfast, he **gets dressed**.
Cuando Ted termina su desayuno, **se viste**.

Then he **washes** his face and hands and **brushes** his teeth.
Luego **se lava** la cara y las manos y **se cepilla** los dientes.

There! Everybody is **ready** now!
¡Ya está! ¡Todo el mundo está **listo**!

Personal hygiene
La higiene personal

Joey's mother puts the **bathroom** in order.
La madre de Joey ordena el **cuarto de baño**.

The bath **towel**.
La **toalla** de baño.

He **combs** his hair.
Él se **peina**.

Mom dries his **hair**.
Mamá le seca el **pelo**.

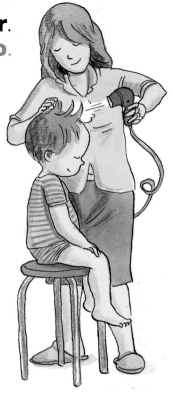

Then she cleans his ears and trims his **nails**.
Luego le limpia las orejas y le corta las **uñas**.

And finally, a touch
of **cologne**!
Y por último, ¡un toque
de **colonia**!

Clothes
La ropa

Shigéru **gets dressed** every morning.
Shigéru **se viste** todas las mañanas.

When it is raining, he wears his **boots** and **raincoat**.
Cuando llueve se pone **botas** e **impermeable**.

A **sweatshirt**.
Una **camisa de entrenamiento**.

He ties the **laces** of his shoes before going out.
Antes de salir, anuda los **lazos** de sus zapatos.

The **shoes**.
Los **zapatos**.

It has snowed;
he must wear
gloves
and a hat.
Ha nevado;
tiene que
ponerse
guantes
y un gorro.

Melvin just got up. He is **hungry**.

Melvin se acaba de levantar. Tiene **hambre**.

Breakfast
El desayuno

Bread and **butter**.
Pan y **mantequilla**.

Mom gives him some orange **juice**.

Mamá le da un **jugo** de naranja.

Then he eats
some **cereal**.
Luego come
cereal.

A glass of **milk**.
Un vaso de **leche**.

He finishes breakfast
with some **fruit**.
Termina el desayuno
con algo de **fruta**.

To go to bed

Irse a dormir

Anthony is **tired**! It's time to go to bed!

Anthony está **cansado**.

Es hora de irse a dormir.

Anthony drinks a small **glass** of water.

Anthony bebe un **vasito** de agua.

Dad always reads him a **story**.
Papá siempre le lee un **cuento**.

A **kiss** for Mom,
a kiss for Dad.
Un **beso** para mamá,
un beso para papá.

Good night!
¡**Buenas noches**!

Aunt Rose and Lalie want to **cook**. First they have to find the cookbook.
La tía Rose y Lalie quieren **cocinar**. Primero deben encontrar el libro de recetas.

To cook
Cocinar

The **cookbook**.
El **libro de recetas**.

Lalie checks that all the **ingredients** are there!
Lalie comprueba de que estén todos los **ingredientes**.

When the **batter** is ready, they
have to pour it into a mold.
Cuando la **mezcla** está lista,
hay que verterla en un molde.

Then they have to
check the **baking**.
Luego hay que vigilar
la **cocción**.

Oh! What a
tasty **muffin**!
¡Oh! ¡Qué **panecillo**
tan rico!

To set the table
Poner la mesa

First we put the **tablecloth**.
Primero ponemos el **mantel**.

Then we put the **dishes**.
Después ponemos los **platos**.

Each **utensil** in its place.
Cada **cubierto** en su sitio.

Mom checks that the **glasses** are clean.
Mamá comprueba que las **copas** estén limpias.

Utensils: **fork**, **knife**, and **spoon**.
Los cubiertos: **tenedor**, **cuchillo** y **cuchara**.

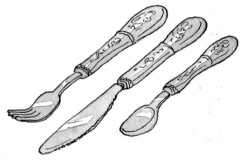

All the **guests** have arrived.
Todos los **invitados** han llegado.

Rosy likes **helping** her mom do the cleaning.
A Rosy le gusta **ayudar** a su mamá a limpiar la casa.

To clean the house
Limpiar la casa

The **broom**.
La **escoba**.

They have to **clean** all the glass.
Deben **limpiar** todos los vidrios.

They **dust** the furniture.
Sacan el polvo a los muebles.

Mom **mops** the floor.
Mamá **pasa la fregona**
por el suelo.

Finally, they
air the house.
Por último,
ventilan toda
la casa.

Ivan loves **drawing**.
A Iván le encanta **dibujar**.

To draw, to cut...

Dibujar, recortar...

He **paints** very carefully.
Pinta con mucho cuidado.

A box of color **pencils**.
Una caja de **lápices** de colores.

Time to **cut out** the figures.
Ahora hay que **recortar** las figuras.

Now to **glue**
the figures together.
Ahora hay que
pegar las figuras.

Ivan is proud of his
masterpiece!
Iván está orgulloso
de su **obra
de arte**.

Jobs
Oficios

Angela's mother is a **hairdresser**.
La mamá de Ángela es **peluquera**.

Her dad is a **mailman**.
Su papá es **cartero**.

Angela is proud of her uncle John, because he owns a **pet shop**.
Ángela está orgullosa de su tío John, porque es dueño de una **tienda de animales**.

Aunt Veronica works in a **bank**.
La tía Verónica trabaja en un **banco**.

Angela's big sister would like to be an air **hostess**.
La hermana mayor de Ángela quisiera ser **azafata**.

But Angela will be a **vet**!
¡Pero Ángela será **veterinaria**!

Yukiko gets his **bag** ready every morning.
Yukiko prepara su **bolsón** todas las mañanas.

School

La escuela

He likes to **wait for** his friends on the way to school.
Le gusta **esperar a** sus amigos camino a la escuela.

The hardest exercise is **dictation**.
El ejercicio más difícil es el **dictado**.

His **teacher**'s
name is Alice.
Su **maestra**
se llama Alice.

Yukiko likes to write on the
blackboard.
A Yukiko le gusta escribir
en la **pizarra**.

During **recess**, he plays
soccer with his friends.
En el **recreo** juega al fútbol
con sus compañeros.

A birthday party
Una fiesta de cumpleaños

Today Loly is five **years** old. She has invited her friends.

Hoy Loly cumple cinco **años**. Ha invitado a sus amigos.

She has planned some **games**.

Ella ha planeado algunos **juegos**.

Now it's time to have some **birthday** cake!
¡Es hora de comer la torta de **cumpleaños**!

The **cake**.
La **torta**.

Loly blows out the **candles**.
Loly sopla las **velas**.

Then she **opens** her presents!
Luego **abre** los regalos.

A new baby at home

Un nuevo bebé en casa

"Look, it's your **bedroom**!"
¡Mira, éste es tu **cuarto**!

Louise wants to lend the baby her **toys**.
Louise quiere prestarle sus **juguetes** al bebé.

A **newborn baby**.
Un **recién nacido**.

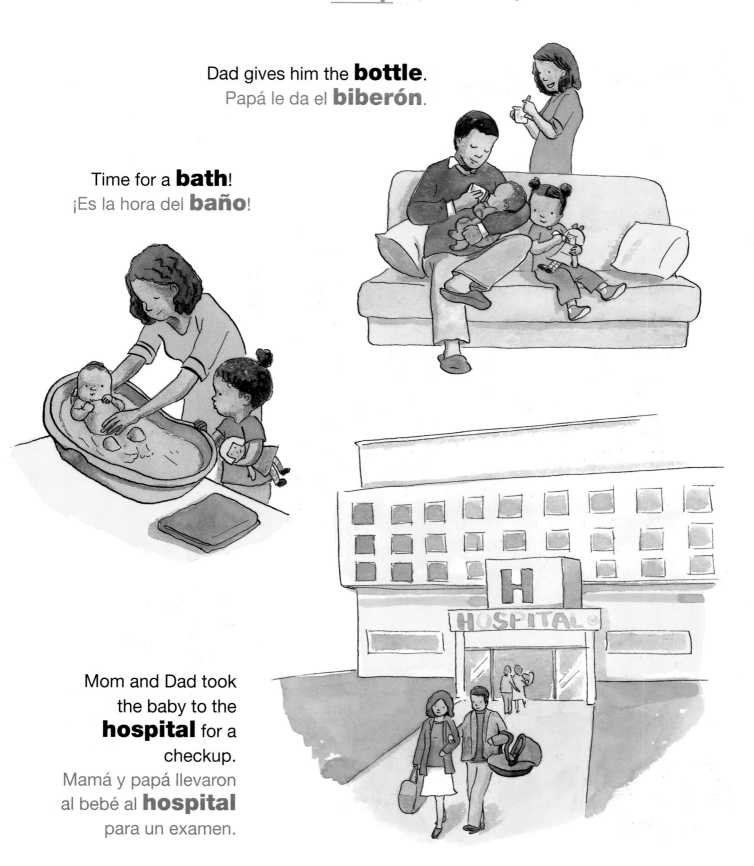

Dad gives him the **bottle**.
Papá le da el **biberón**.

Time for a **bath**!
¡Es la hora del **baño**!

Mom and Dad took the baby to the **hospital** for a checkup.
Mamá y papá llevaron al bebé al **hospital** para un examen.

Games
Juegos

On Sunday, Harold plays **cards** with his brother and his grandfather.

Los domingos Harold juega a las **cartas** con su hermano y su abuelito.

A game of **checkers**.

Un juego de **damas**.

He plays **video games**.

Juega a los **video juegos.**

Harold plays **marbles**
in the school playground.
En el patio de la escuela,
Harold juega a las **canicas**.

Arghhhh! I am the **wolf**
and I will eat you up!
¡Ahhhhhh! ¡Soy el **lobo**
y te voy a comer!

The girls skip
rope.
Las niñas
juegan a saltar
a la **cuerda**.

Mark and his dad watch the cars at the **toy store**.
En la **juguetería**, Mark y su padre miran los carros.

Toys

Juguetes

He is the **fastest** riding his car!
¡Es el más **rápido** en su carro!

Mark likes playing with his **action toys**.
A Mark le gusta mucho jugar con sus **figuras de acción**.

His kid sister, Amy, plays **shopping** with her friends.
Su hermanita Amy juega a **las compras** con sus amigas.

She plays with her favorite **fluffy toys** on her bed.
Ella juega en la cama con sus **peluches** preferidos.

Watch out! That's my **super-fast car**!
¡Cuidado! ¡Ese es mi **coche superrápido**!

The body | El cuerpo

The **parts** of the body.
Las **partes** del cuerpo.

head / cabeza

arm / brazo

hand / mano

belly / vientre

leg / pierna

knee / rodilla

foot / pie

little finger / meñique
ring finger / anular
middle finger / corazón
index finger / índice
thumb / pulgar

The **hand**.
La **mano**.

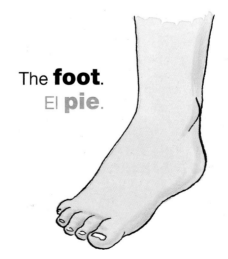

The **foot**.
El **pie**.

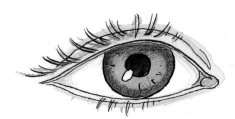

The **eye**.
El **ojo**.

Greg **has grown** a lot, but he will always be smaller than his nephew.
Greg **ha crecido** mucho, pero siempre será más pequeño que su primo.

Every year the doctor checks Peter to make sure he is in good **health**.
Todos los años la doctora revisa a Peter para asegurar que tenga buena **salud**.

The **five** senses.
Los **cinco** sentidos.

sight / la vista   hearing / la audición

smell / el olfato   taste / el gusto

touch / el tacto

Senses
Los sentidos

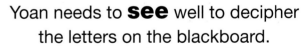

Yoan needs to **see** well to decipher the letters on the blackboard.
Yoan necesita tener buena **vista** para descifrar las letras de la pizarra.

He sometimes **tastes** new foods.
A veces **prueba** nuevas comidas.

To recognize his friend, Jimmy, he has to **touch** his face.
Para reconocer a su amigo Jimmy, tiene que **tocarle** la cara.

This perfume **smells** good!
¡Este perfume **huele** bien!

The teacher is going to play the tambourine. Yoan **listens**.
La maestra va a tocar la pandereta. Yoan **escucha**.

Joseph is very **mad**;
somebody broke his car.
Joseph está muy
enfadado; alguien
rompió su carro.

Feelings
Los sentimientos

He is **adorable**!
¡Es **adorable**!

Mom spends a lot of time with the baby.
Joseph is a little **jealous**.
Mamá pasa mucho tiempo con el bebé.
Joseph está un poco **celoso**.

He is very **happy**;
his team has won!
Está muy
contento; ¡su
equipo ha ganado!

Joseph is **sad**; his balloon
has gone up in the air.
Joseph está **triste** porque
se le voló el globo.

Ron's chocolate **looks good**!
¡**Qué bien luce** el chocolate de Ron!

Sports

Deportes

Alicia plays **volleyball** at school.
En la escuela Alicia juega **vóleibol**.

Afterwards she plays **tennis**.
Después juega **tenis**.

Her brother plays **soccer**.
Su hermano juega al **fútbol**.

When she was on vacation, she went **ice-skating** with her big sister.
Durante las vacaciones fue a **patinar sobre el hielo** con su hermana mayor.

He likes **baseball** best.
Él prefiere jugar **béisbol**.

Their father teaches them how to play **golf** on weekends.
Los fines de semana su padre les enseña a jugar **golf**.

To dance, to sing...
Bailar, cantar...

Elizabeth loves dancing and **singing**. She practices a lot!

A Elizabeth le encanta bailar y **cantar**. ¡Practica mucho!

Alicia dances **ballet** every Wednesday.

Alicia baila **ballet** todos los miércoles.

At the end of the year there will be a **dancing** show.

A final de año habrá un espectáculo de **danza**.

At her aunt's wedding, she danced a **waltz**.

En la boda de su tía bailó el **vals**.

She makes up **songs** in her bedroom.

Ella inventa **canciones** en su dormitorio.

For her birthday, her parents gave her a ticket for a **concert**.

Para su cumpleaños, sus padres le regalaron una entrada para un **concierto**.

Musical instruments
Instrumentos musicales

Davis plays the **flute**.
Davis toca la **flauta**.

A **guitar**.
Una **guitarra**.

His sister Lucy is studying **piano**.
Su hermana Lucy
está aprendiendo **piano**.

Their father is a great **sax** player.
Su padre es un gran intérprete de **saxo**.

An **accordion**.
Un **acordeón**.

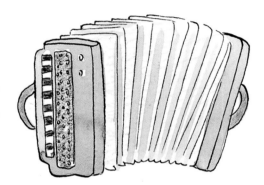

Sometimes they all play together and Mom **sings** along.
A veces tocan todos juntos y la mamá **canta**.

A **strawberry**.
Una **fresa**.

Fruits
Frutas

At the end of summer, Jane and Harmony pick **apples**.
Al final del verano, Jane y Harmony recogen **manzanas**.

They help their grandma to make **marmalade**.
Ayudan a su abuelita a hacer **mermelada**.

When it is cold, Mom makes juice from freshly pressed **oranges**.

Cuando hace frío, mamá prepara jugo de **naranjas** recién exprimidas.

Jane loves fruit **pies**.

A Jane le gustan los **pasteles** de frutas.

In September it is **harvest** time!

¡En septiembre se hace la **cosecha**!

Vegetables
Las verduras

Kimi often goes to the **market**
with her mom.
Kimi a menudo va al **mercado**
con su mamá.

A **basket**
with vegetables.
Una **cesta**
de verduras.

There are **pumpkins** growing
in Grandpa's garden.
En el huerto del abuelito crecen
calabazas.

Kimi picks some **tomatoes** also.
Kimi recoge algunos **tomates** también.

Mom puts some **leeks**, **carrots**, and **potatoes** in the soup.
Mamá pone **puerros**, **zanahorias** y **papas** en la sopa.

Vegetables are **good** for your health!
¡Las verduras son **buenas** para la salud!

Sweets, candies...
Dulces, caramelos...

At the fair, Elise had some **cotton candy**.

En la feria, Elise come **algodón de azúcar**.

Candy.
Caramelos.

At the movies, Elise and her friends have **popcorn** and **lollipops**.

En el cine, Elise y sus amigas comen **palomitas** y **chupetes**.

In summer, at the beach,
Elise **licks** an ice cream.
En verano, en la playa,
Elise **lame** un helado.

An **ice cream**.
Un **helado**.

¡What a good
dessert!
¡Qué bueno es
este **postre**!

Amelia loves **wildflowers**.
A Amelia le encantan las **flores silvestres**.

Flowers
Flores

She presents a **bouquet** in the evening.
Por la tarde ella regala un **ramo** de flores.

A **sunflower**.
Un **girasol**.

In Holland they visited the **tulip** gardens.
En Holanda visitaron los campos de **tulipanes**.

You have to put them in a **vase** with water.
Hay que ponerlas en un **jarrón** con agua.

The **iris**.
Los **lirios**.

It's funny, the **sun** makes a big shadow on the sand!
¡Qué divertido! El **sol** hace una sombra grande en la arena.

This planet is **Saturn**.
Este planeta es **Saturno**.

The sky
El cielo

Rose and Nils love watching the **stars** at night in summer.
A Rose y a Nils les gusta mucho observar las **estrellas** en las noches de verano.

The **moon** is waning tonight.
Esta noche la **luna** está en menguante.

Nils watches through the **telescope**.
Nils observa a través del **telescopio**.

They often go with Grandpa to admire the **sunset**.
A menudo van con el abuelito a admirar la **puesta de sol**.

Seasons
Las estaciones

Kelly picks flowers for her mom when it's **spring**.
En **primavera** Kelly recoge flores para su mamá.

Quick, the **storm** is about to break out. We should look for shelter.
Rápido, la **tormenta** ya llega. Hay que cobijarse.

Kelly goes to the beach in **summer**.
En **verano**, Kelly va a la playa.

This **bunny** will soon go back to its den to hibernate! ¡Este **conejito** pronto volverá a su madriguera para hibernar!

It's **fall**. Kelly gathers leaves and chestnuts for her teacher.
Es **otoño**. Kelly recoge hojas y castañas para la maestra.

It's **winter**! Kelly is making a snowman.
¡Es **invierno**! Kelly hace un muñeco de nieve.

Surya loves **picnics**.
A Surya le encantan las **meriendas campestres**.

A picnic

Un día de campo

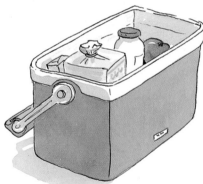

The **cooler**.
La **nevera**.

Nassim helps Grandma take out the **food**.
Nassim ayuda a la abuelita a sacar la **comida**.

Grandpa and Dad have already prepared their **fishing rods**.
El abuelito y papá ya han preparado sus **cañas de pescar**.

While they wait for lunch, Surya and Nassim play **badminton**.
Mientras esperan el almuerzo, Surya y Nassim juegan al **bádminton**.

And now it is time to **eat**!
¡Y ya es hora de **comer**!

The beach
La playa

Timothy impatiently awaits his vacation by the **sea**.
Timothy espera con impaciencia sus vacaciones en el **mar**.

Mom does not forget to apply **sunblock**.
Mamá no se olvida de la **crema protectora**.

Water is **great**!
¡El agua está **estupenda**!

He goes **diving** with his dad.
Él **bucea** con su papá.

Later on he plays with the **wooden paddles**.
Después juega con las **paletas de madera**.

He and his little sister look for **shells**.
Con su hermanita buscan **conchas**.

Pets and mascots
Mascotas diversas

When Oliver was little, he was never far from his **favorite object**.

Cuando Oliver era pequeño, no se separaba nunca de su **objeto preferido**.

Now he keeps the **key holder** his dad brought him from a trip.

Ahora lleva el **llavero** que papá le trajo de un viaje.

The basketball game is over. Oliver hugs the team's **mascot**.

El partido de baloncesto ha terminado. Oliver abraza a la **mascota** del equipo.

A **turtle**.
Una **tortuga**.

Oliver has a small **hamster**, his name is Micky.
Oliver tiene un **hámster** pequeño que se llama Micky.

Farm animals
Los animales de granja

The **duck** and
the ducklings.
La **pata** y los
patitos.

Elsa is on **vacation** at
Aunt Carrie's farm.
Elsa está de **vacaciones** en
la granja de su tía Carrie.

They feed and give water
to the **cows**.
Ellas les dan de comer
y beber a las **vacas**.

They have to take care of the **pigs** too.
También tienen que ocuparse de los **cerdos**.

The big **rabbit** eats a carrot.
El **conejo** grande come una zanahoria.

The **little lambs** are so cute!
¡Qué bonitos son los **corderitos**!

The aquarium
El acuario

Luc and his dad have a nice **fish tank** at home.
Luc y su padre tienen una hermosa **pecera** en casa.

Luc also has a small **red fish**.
Luc también tiene un **pececito rojo**.

Today they are going to choose a new **fish**.
Hoy van a escoger un **pez** nuevo.

They go to the oceanographic **museum** every year.
Todos los años van al **museo** oceanográfico.

A **yellow fish**.
Un **pez amarillo**.

This one will not go into the fish tank. They will throw it back into the **water**!
Éste no irá a la pecera.
¡Lo devolverán al **agua**!

Insects

Insectos

George's grandfather **collects** insects.
El abuelo de George **colecciona** insectos.

A **grasshopper**.
Un **saltamontes**.

They found an **anthill** in the woods.
En el bosque encontraron un **hormiguero**.

They look for **dragonflies** around the pond.
Buscan **libélulas** al borde del estanque.

George takes good care of his **insects**.
George cuida bien sus **insectos**.

The beautiful **butterfly**!
¡La hermosa **mariposa**!

Birds
Aves

On vacation by the sea,
Mary admires the **seagulls**.
De vacaciones en el mar,
Mary admira las **gaviotas**.

A **nest**.
Un **nido**.

Grandpa fills the **feeder**
with small seeds.
El abuelito rellena el **comedero**
con semillitas.

Grandpa's **parrot** can
say: "Hello Mary!"
El **loro** del abuelito sabe
decir: "¡Hola Mary!"

At the zoo, Dad
takes a picture
of the **pelicans**.
En el zoológico, papá
toma una foto a los
pelícanos.

In the evening they put
the **geese** inside.
Al anochecer hay que
entrar a los **gansos**.

Animals of the forest
Animales del bosque

Walking through the woods, we have seen a **deer**.

Paseando por el bosque, hemos visto un **ciervo**.

Oh! A beautiful **squirrel**!

¡Oh! ¡Qué **ardilla** tan bonita!

Badgers.
Los **tejones**.

The **owl** is trying to sleep.
La **lechuza** intenta dormir.

A **fox** is hidden inside a tree trunk!
¡Un **zorro** se ha escondido
en un tronco de árbol!

A visit to the zoo
Una visita al zoológico

Today Mom and Dad take Ron and Alan to the **zoo**.
Hoy mamá y papá llevan a Ron y Alan al **zoológico**.

They want to watch the seal **show**.
Quieren ver el **espectáculo** de las focas.

Inside an enclosed ring they may touch the little **goats**.
En un pequeño cercado pueden acariciar a las **cabritas**.

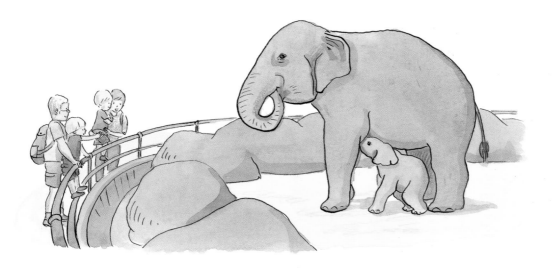

Ron calls out the little **elephant's** mother.
Ron llama a la mamá del pequeño **elefante**.

A **gorilla**.
Un **gorila**.

In front of the wild animals,
Alan imitates the **lion**!
Delante de la jaula de las fieras,
Alan imita al **león**.

Pablo and Soledad go to the **amusement park** with their parents.

Pablo y Soledad van al **parque de diversiones** con sus padres.

The fun fair

El parque de diversiones

The **roller coaster**.
La **montaña rusa**.

Pablo and Soledad love the **floating tree trunk**.

A Pablo y Soledad les gusta mucho el **tronco flotante**.

But what they like best is the
inflatable castle!
¡Pero lo que más les gusta es el
castillo inflable!

The **Ferris wheel**.
La **rueda gigante**.

Careful, the plane
is about to take off!
¡Atención, el
avión va a despegar!

The circus
El circo

Margaret and her dad go to the **circus**!
¡Margaret y su papá van al **circo**!

The big **tiger** is jumping through the fire hoop.
El gran **tigre** salta por el aro de fuego.

The **seal** and its ball.
La **foca** y su pelota.

The big **tent**.
La gran **carpa**.

The **acrobat**
is very skilled.
La **acróbata**
es muy hábil.

Margaret likes
the **clown**
show very much.
A Margaret
le encanta
el espectáculo
del **payaso**.

Fancy or funny dresses

Trajes finos o divertidos

Lisa dreams of wearing her aunt's **wedding gown**.
Lisa sueña con llevar el **vestido de novia** de su tía.

For her birthday, Lucy got a beautiful **princess** dress.
Para su cumpleaños, a Lucy le regalaron un hermoso vestido de **princesa**.

For carnival, Lisa wore a **crocodile** costume.
Para carnaval, Lisa se disfrazó de **cocodrilo**.

Mom and Dad often invite their friend Roger. He is very **funny** as a clown!
Mamá y papá a menudo invitan a su amigo Roger. ¡Es muy **divertido** como payaso!

Dad brought a funny **hat** from his trip.
Papá trajo un **sombrero** divertido de su viaje.

Mom has taken the girls to a **fashion show**.
Mamá ha llevado a las niñas a un **desfile de modas**.

Scary or cute costumes

Disfraces lindos o miedosos

During the ghost ride, Grace and Jim had a big scare with the **skeleton**!

En el tren fantasma, Grace y Jim se asustaron mucho con el **esqueleto**.

Grace was very impressed in front of the **witch**!

¡Delante de la **bruja**, Grace se sintió muy impresionada!

Grace plays
ghosts with
her cousins.
Grace juega a los
fantasmas
con sus primos.

Grace is disguised as a **fairy**!
¡Grace se ha disfrazado de **hada**!

Jim has made himself a
monster **costume**.
Jim se ha hecho un disfraz
de **monstruo**.

Christmas

Navidad

Tomorrow is **Christmas**! Igor and Ania can hardly wait!

Mañana es **Navidad**.

¡Igor y Ania ya no aguantan más!

Santa Claus.
Papá Noel.

Grandparents arrive for Christmas **dinner**.

Los abuelos llegan para la **cena** navideña.

Before going to bed, the children hang their **stockings** from the chimney.

Antes de irse a dormir, los niños cuelgan los **calcetines** en la chimenea.

The **presents**.
Los **regalos**.

Santa Claus **has come**!

¡El Papá Noel **ha venido**!

Characters from famous stories

Pesonajes de cuentos famosos

In his bedroom Harry has a poster of his hero, **Peter Pan**.

En su dormitorio Harry tiene un póster de su héroe, **Peter Pan**.

In the merry-go-round, Mary always chooses the **Ugly Duckling**.

En el carrusel Mary siempre elige al **Patito Feo**.

Snow White.
Blancanieves.

When Mary invites her friends, they play **Cinderella**.

Cuando Mary invita a sus amigas, juegan a la **Cenicienta**.

Mary loves it when Grandpa reads **Little Red Riding Hood** to her.

A Mary le gusta que su abuelito le lea el cuento de la **Caperucita Roja**.

Harry went to the movies to see **Goldilocks**.

Harry fue al cine a ver **Ricitos de Oro**.

Martin takes the **bus** to go to school every morning.
Todas las mañanas, Martín toma el **autobús** para ir a la escuela.

The **plane**.
El **avión**.

Transportation
El transporte

Martin rides in the **car** to go visit Grandpa and Grandma.
Martín va en **carro** a visitar a sus abuelitos.

They are taking
the **train** today.
Hoy toman
el **tren**.

Martin watches the **ships** go by.
Martín mira pasar los **barcos**.

On Sunday he goes
biking with his dad.
Los domingos **va en**
bicicleta con su papá.

The beauty parlor
El salón de belleza

Today Olivia and her mom have an appointment at the **beauty parlor**.

Hoy Olivia y su mamá tienen hora en el **salón de belleza**.

Hair **shampooing**.
El **lavado** del cabello.

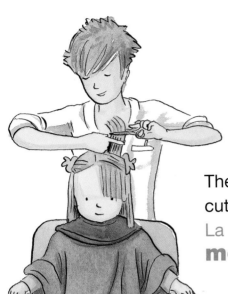

The **comb** and the **scissors**.
El **peine** y las **tijeras**.

The hairdresser
cuts the first **locks of hair**.
La peluquera corta los primeros
mechones de pelo.

Mom waits for her hair **to dry**.
Mamá espera que se le **seque** el pelo.

Olivia finds herself **pretty**!
¡Olivia se encuentra **bonita**!

The doctor
El médico

Mom takes Arthur to the **doctor** this morning.
Esta mañana, mamá lleva a Arthur al **médico**.

He places Arthur on the **examination table**.
El médico coloca a Arthur sobre la **camilla**.

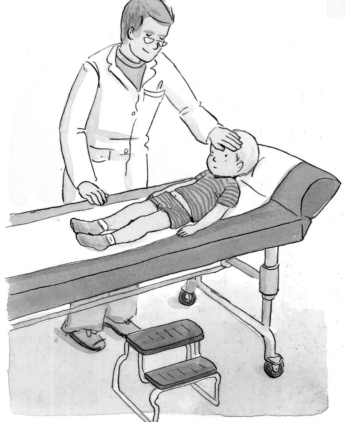

The **stethoscope**.
El **estetoscopio**.

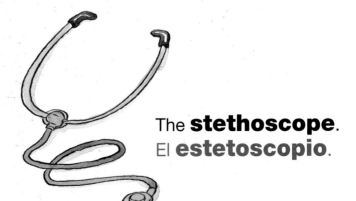

He **weighs** and
measures him.
Lo **pesa** y
lo **mide**.

He listens to his **heartbeat**.
Le escucha el **latido del
corazón**.

It's just
a touch of **flu**!
¡Sólo tiene un
poco de **gripe**!

Frank likes
going to
the **park**.
A Frank le gusta
ir al **parque**.

The park
El parque

He likes **riding**
the rocking car.
Le gusta **montarse**
en el coche-balancín.

He **meets** his friends there.
Allí se **encuentra** con
sus amigos.

He makes **sand** castles for his little sister.
Hace castillos de **arena** para su hermanita.

What I like the best is the **swing**.
Lo que más me gusta es el **columpio**.

The **toboggan** is for older kids!
¡El **tobogán** es para los niños mayores!

The supermarket

El supermercado

Nelson likes to go **shopping**.
A Nelson le gusta ir a **hacer las compras**.

He **chooses** breakfast cereal.
Elige su cereal para desayuno.

He likes to read by the **magazine rack**.
Le gusta leer en la **sección de revistas**.

At the **fish section** he always watches the crabs.
En la **pescadería** siempre mira los cangrejos.

Salt, pepper… Dad checks his **list** so he won't forget anything!
Sal, pimienta… papá repasa la **lista** para no olvidarse de nada.

Now you have to go to the **checkout counter**!
¡Ahora hay que pasar por la **caja**!

Chuck will catch
a plane **today**.
Chuck va a tomar
un avión **hoy**.

Airport
El aeropuerto

The planes on the **runway**
are getting ready to take off.
En la **pista**, los aviones se
preparan para despegar.

He is impressed. The **airport** is very large.
Está impresionado. El **aeropuerto**
es muy grande.

Chuck goes to the **check-in** counter with his dad.
Chuk acompaña a su papá a **facturar** las maletas.

In the plane you must fasten your **seat belt**.
En el avión hay que abrocharse el **cinturón**.

There! The plane is **taking off**!
¡Ya está! ¡El avión está **despegando**!

To introduce a person
Presentar a alguien

My name is
Peter, what's yours?
Me llamo Peter,
¿cómo te llamas tú?

Will you **play with me**?
My name is Dan and this is my friend Julia.
¿Quieres **jugar conmigo**?
Me llamo Dan y esta es mi amiga Julia.

I really like your shirt.
Where did you get it?
Me gusta mucho tu camisa.
¿Dónde la compraste?

My **friend** Lola.
Mi **amiga** Lola.

You and your
friends are having
a lot of fun.
Can I play too?
My name is Sam.
Tú y tus amigos
están divirtiéndose
mucho. ¿**Puedo
jugar yo
también**?
Me llamo Sam.

Let's go over!

¡Vamos a repasar!

House / La casa p.4

Home: casa

Living room: salón

Garden: jardín

Bed: cama

Garage: garaje

Desk: escritorio

Family / La familia p.6

Little sister: hermanita

Parents: padres

Family: familia

Cousins: primos

Aunt: tía

Grandpa: abuelo

Grandma: abuela

Time to get up / Hora de levantarse p.8

Alarm clock: despertador

Hug: abrazo

Having breakfast: desayunando

Get dressed: se viste

Washes: se lava

Brushes: se cepilla

Ready: listo

Personal hygiene / La higiene personal p.10

Bathroom: cuarto de baño

Towel: toalla

Comb: peine

Hair: pelo

Nails: uñas

Cologne: colonia

Clothes / La ropa p.12

Morning: mañanas

Sweatshirt: sudadera

Boots: botas

Raincoat: impermeable

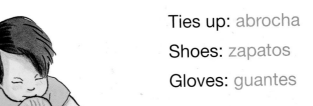

Ties up: abrocha

Shoes: zapatos

Gloves: guantes

Breakfast / El desayuno

Hungry: hambre
Bread: pan
Butter: mantequilla
Juice: jugo
Cereal: cereal
Milk: leche
Fruit: fruta

To go to bed / Irse a dormir

Tired: cansado
Brushes: cepilla
Glass: vasito
Story: cuento
Kiss: beso
Good night!: ¡Buenas noches!

To cook / Cocinar

To cook: cocinar
Cookbook: libro de recetas
Ingredients: ingredientes
Batter: mezcla
Baking: cocción
Muffin: panecillo

To set the table / Poner la mesa p.20

Tablecloth: mantel

Dishes: platos

Utensil: cubierto

Glasses: copas

Fork: tenedor

Knife: cuchillo

Spoon: cuchara

Guests: invitados

To clean the house / Limpiar la casa p.22

Helping: ayudar

Broom: escoba

Clean: limpiar

Dust: sacan el polvo

Mops: pasa la fregona

Air: ventilan

To draw, to cut... / Dibujar, recortar... . . . . . . p.24

Drawing: dibujar

Paints: pinta

Pencils: lápices

Cut out: recortar

Glue: pegar

Masterpiece: obra de arte

Jobs / Oficios p.26

Hairdresser: peluquera

Mailman: cartero

Pet shop: tienda de animales

Bank: banco

Hostess: azafata

Vet: veterinaria

School / Escuela p.28

Bag: bolsón

Wait for: esperar a

Dictation: dictado

Teacher: maestra

Blackboard: pizarra

Recess: recreo

A birthday party / Una fiesta de cumpleaños p.30

Years: años

Games: juegos

Birthday: cumpleaños

Cake: torta

Candles: velas

Opens: abre

A new baby at home / Un nuevo bebé en casa . p.32

Bedroom: cuarto

Toys: juguetes

Newborn baby: recién nacido

Bottle: biberón

Bath: baño

Checkup: examen

Games / Juegos p.34

Cards: cartas

Checkers: damas

Video games: video juegos

Marbles: canicas

Wolf: lobo

Rope: cuerda

Toys / Juguetes p.36

Toy store: juguetería

Fastest: el más rápido

Action toys: figuras de acción

Shopping: compras

Fluffy toys: peluches

Super-fast car: coche superrápido

The body / El cuerpo p.38

Parts: partes

Hand: mano

Foot: pie

Eye: ojo

Grown: crecido

Health: salud

Senses / Los sentidos . . p.40

Five: cinco

Sight: vista

Tastes: prueba

Touch: tocar

Smells: huele

Listens: escucha

Feelings / Los sentimientos p.42

Mad: enfadado

Adorable: adorable

Jealous: celoso

Happy: contento

Sad: triste

Looks good!: ¡Qué bien luce!

Sports / Deportes

Volleyball: vóleibol

Tennis: tenis

Soccer: fútbol

Ice-skating: patinar sobre el hielo

Baseball: béisbol

Golf: golf

To dance, to sing... / Bailar, cantar...

Singing: cantar

Ballet: ballet

Dancing: danza

Waltz: vals

Songs: canciones

Concert: concierto

Musical instruments / Instrumentos musicales

Flute: flauta

Guitar: guitarra

Piano: piano

Sax: saxo

Accordion: acordeón

Sings: canta

Fruits / Frutas p.50

Strawberry: fresa

Apples: manzanas

Marmalade: mermelada

Oranges: naranjas

Pies: pasteles

Harvest: cosecha

Vegetables / Las verduras p.52

Market: mercado

Basket: cesta

Pumpkins: calabazas

Tomatoes: tomates

Leeks: puerros

Potatoes: papas

Carrots: zanahorias

Good: buenas

Sweets, candies... / Dulces, caramelos... . . . . p.54

Cotton candy: algodón de azúcar

Candy: caramelos

Popcorn: palomitas

Lollipops: chupetes

Licks: lame

Ice cream: helado

Dessert: postre

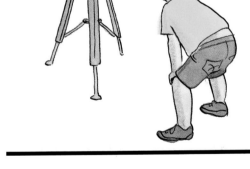

A picnic / Un día de campo p.62

Picnics: meriendas campestres

Cooler: nevera

Food: comida

Fishing rods: cañas de pescar

Badminton: bádminton

Eat: comer

The beach / La playa p.64

Sea: mar

Sunblock: crema protectora

Great: estupenda

Diving: bucear

Wooden paddles: paletas de madera

Shells: conchas

Pets and mascots / Mascotas diversas p.66

Favorite object: objeto preferido

Key holder: llavero

Mascot: mascota

Turtle: tortuga

Hamster: hámster

Farm animals / Los animales de granja p.68

Duck: pato

Vacation: vacaciones

Cows: vacas

Pigs: cerdos

Rabbit: conejo

Little lambs: corderitos

The aquarium / El acuario p.70

Fish tank: pecera

Red fish: pececito rojo

Fish: pez

Museum: museo

Yellow fish: pez amarillo

Water: agua

Insects / Insectos . . p.72

Collects: colecciona

Grasshopper: saltamontes

Anthill: hormiguero

Dragonflies: libélulas

Insects: insectos

Butterfly: mariposa

Birds / Aves p.74

Seagulls: gaviotas

Nest: nido

Feeder: comedero

Parrot: loro

Pelicans: pelícanos

Geese: gansos

Animals of the forest / Animales del bosque p.76

Deer: ciervo

Squirrel: ardilla

Badgers: tejones

Owl: lechuza

Fox: zorro

A visit to the zoo / Una visita al zoológico . . . p.78

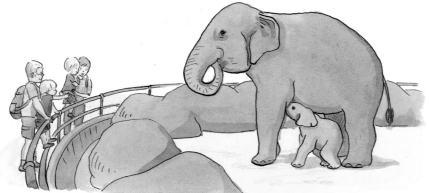

Zoo: zoológico

Show: espectáculo

Goats: cabritas

Elephant: elefante

Gorilla: gorila

Lion: león

The fun fair / El parque de diversiones p.80

Amusement park: parque de diversiones

Roller coaster: montaña rusa

Floating tree trunk: tronco flotante

Inflatable castle: castillo inflable

Ferris wheel: rueda gigante

Careful: atención

The circus / El circo p.82

Circus: circo

Seal: foca

Tiger: tigre

Tent: carpa

Acrobat: acróbata

Clown: payaso

Fancy or funny dresses / Trajes finos o divertidos p.84

Wedding gown: vestido de novia

Princess: princesa

Crocodile: cocodrilo

Funny: divertido

Hat: sombrero

Fashion show: desfile de modas

Scary or cute costumes / Disfraces lindos o miedosos p.86

Skeleton: esqueleto
Witch: bruja
Ghosts: fantasmas
Fairy: hada
Monster: monstruo

Christmas / Navidad p.88

Christmas: Navidad
Santa Claus: Papá Noel
Dinner: cena
Stockings: calcetines
Presents: regalos
Has come: ha venido

Characters from stories / Personajes de cuentos. . p.90

Peter Pan: Peter Pan
Ugly Duckling: Patito feo
Snow White: Blancanieves
Cinderella: Cenicienta

Little Red Riding Hood: Caperucita Roja
Goldilocks: Ricitos de Oro

Transportation / El transporte p.92

Bus: autobús

Plane: avión

Car: carro

Train: tren

Ships: barcos

Biking: va en bicicleta

The beauty parlor / El salón de belleza p.94

Appointment: tienen hora

Shampooing: lavado

Comb: peine

Scissors: tijeras

Locks of hair: mechones de pelo

To dry: secar

Pretty: bonita

The doctor / El médico p.96

Doctor: médico

Examination table: camilla

Stethoscope: estetoscopio

Weighs: pesa

Measures: mide

Heartbeat: latido del corazón

Flu: gripe

The park / El parque p.98

Park: parque

Riding: montarse

Meets: encuentra

Sand: arena

Swing: columpio

Toboggan: tobogán

The supermarket / El supermercado p.100

Shopping: hacer las compras

Chooses: elige

Book department: sección de libros

Fish section: pescadería

List: list

Checkout counter: caja

Airport / El aeropuerto p.102

Today: hoy

Runway: pista

Airport: aeropuerto

Check-in: facturar

Seat belt: cinturón

Taking off: despegando

To introduce a person / Presentar a alguien   p.104

My name is: me llamo

Play with me: jugar conmigo

I really like: me gusta mucho

Friend: amiga

Can I play too?: ¿Puedo jugar yo también?

Alphabetical dictionary

A
Accordion: acordeón
Acrobat: acróbata
Action toy: figura de acción
Adorable: adorable
Air: ventilar
Airport: aeropuerto
Alarm clock: despertador
Amusement park: parque de diversiones
Anthill: hormiguero
Apple: manzana
Appointment: cita
Aunt: tía

B
Badger: tejón
Badminton: bádminton
Bag: bolsón
Baking: cocción
Ballet: ballet
Bank: banco
Baseball: béisbol
Basket: cesta
Bath: baño
Bathroom: cuarto de baño
Batter: mezcla
Bed: cama
Bedroom: dormitorio
Bike: bicicleta
Birthday: cumpleaños
Blackboard: pizarra
Book: libro
Boots: botas
Bottle: biberón
Bouquet: ramo
Bread: pan
Breakfast: desayuno
Broom: escoba
Brush: cepillar
Bunny: conejito
Bus: autobús
Butter: mantequilla
Butterfly: mariposa

C
Cake: torta
Candle: vela
Candy: caramelo
Car: carro
Card: tarjeta
Careful: atención
Carrot: zanahoria
Castle: castillo
Cereal: cereal
Check-in: facturar
Checkers: damas
Checkout counter: caja
Christmas: Navidad
Choose: elegir
Cinderella: Cenicienta
Circus: circo
Clean: limpiar
Clown: payaso
Cologne: colonia
Collect: coleccionar
Comb: peine
Come: venir
Concert: concierto
Cousin: primo
Cook: cocinar
Cookbook: libro de recetas
Cooler: nevera
Cotton candy: algodón de azúcar
Cow: vaca
Crocodile: cocodrilo
Cut out: recortar

D
Dance: danzar
Deer: ciervo
Desk: escritorio
Dessert: postre
Dictation: dictado
Dinner: cena
Dish: plato
Dive: bucear
Doctor: médico
Dragonfly: libélula
Draw: dibujar
Dry: secar
Duck: pato
Dust: sacar el polvo

E
Eat: comer
Elephant: elefante
Examination table: camilla
Eye: ojo

F
Fairy: hada
Fall: otoño
Family: familia
Fashion show: desfile de modas
Fast: rápido
Favorite: preferido
Feeder: comedero
Ferris wheel: rueda gigante
Fish: pez
Fish section: pescadería
Fish tank: pecera
Fishing rod: caña de pescar
Five: cinco
Floating tree trunk: tronco flotante
Flu: gripe
Fluffy toy: peluche
Flute: flauta
Food: comida
Foot: pie
Fork: tenedor
Fox: zorro
Friend: amigo
Fruit: fruta
Funny: divertido

G
Game: juego
Garage: garaje
Garden: jardín
Geese: gansos
Get dressed: vestirse
Ghost: fantasma
Glass: vaso, copa
Gloves: guantes
Glue: pegar
Goat: cabra
Goldilocks: Ricitos de Oro
Golf: golf
Good: bueno
Gorilla: gorila
Grandma: abuela
Grandpa: abuelo
Grasshopper: saltamontes
Great: estupenda
Grow: crecer
Guest: invitado
Guitar: guitarra

H
Hair: pelo
Hairdresser: peluquero
Hamster: hámster
Hand: mano
Happy: contento
Harvest: cosecha
Hat: gorro
Health: salud
Heartbeat: latido del corazón
Help: ayudar
Home: casa
Hostess: azafata
Hug: abrazo
Hungry: hambriento

I
Ice cream: helado
Ice-skating: patinar sobre el hielo
Inflatable: inflable
Ingredients: ingredientes
Insect: insecto
Iris: lirio

J
Jealous: celoso
Juice: jugo

K
Key holder: llavero
Kiss: beso
Knife: cuchillo

L
Lamb: cordero
Leek: puerro
Lick: lamer
Like: gustar
Lion: león
List: lista
Listen: escuchar
Little: pequeño
Little Red Riding Hood:
Caperucita Roja
Living room: salón
Lock of hair:
mechón de pelo
Lollipop: chupete
Looks good!:
¡Qué bien luce!

M
Mad: enfadado
Mailman: cartero
Marbles: canicas
Market: mercado
Marmalade: mermelada
Mascot: mascota
Masterpiece:
obra de arte
Measure: medir
Meet: encontrar
Milk: leche
Monster: monstruo
Moon: luna
Mop: pasar la fregona
Morning: mañana
Muffin: panecillo
Museum: museo

N
Nail: uña
Name: nombre
Nest: nido
Newborn baby:
recién nacido
Night: noche

O
Open: abrir
Orange: naranja
Owl: lechuza

P
Paint: pintar
Parents: padres
Park: parque
Parrot: loro
Part: parte
Pelican: pelícano
Pencil: lápiz
Pet shop:
tienda de animales
Peter Pan: Peter Pan
Piano: piano
Picnic: merienda campestre
Pie: pastel
Pig: cerdo
Play: jugar
Plane: avión
Popcorn: palomitas
Potato: papa
Present: regalo
Pretty: bonita
Princess: princesa
Pumpkin: calabaza

R
Rabbit: conejo
Raincoat: impermeable
Ready: listo
Recess: recreo
Red: rojo
Ride: montar
Roller coaster:
montaña rusa
Rope: cuerda
Runway: pista

S
Sad: triste
Sand: arena
Santa Claus: Papá Noel
Saturn: Saturno
Sax: saxo
Scissors: tijeras

Seal: foca
Star: estrella
Sea: mar
Seagull: gaviota
Seat belt: cinturón
See: ver
Sell: vender
Shampooing: lavado
Shell: concha
Ship: barco
Shoes: zapatos
Shopping: compras
Show: espectáculo
Sing: cantar
Sister: hermana
Skeleton: esqueleto
Smell: oler
Snow White: Blancanieves
Soccer: fútbol
Sock: calcetín
Song: canción
Spoon: cuchara
Spring: primavera
Squirrel: ardilla
Stethoscope:
estetoscopio
Storm: tormenta
Story: cuento
Strawberry: fresa
Summer: verano
Sun: sol
Sunblock: crema
protectora
Sunflower: girasol
Sunset: puesta de sol
Super-fast car: coche
superrápido
Sweatshirt: sudadera
Swing: columpio

T
Tablecloth: mantel
Take off: despegar
Taste: probar
Teacher: maestra
Teeth: dientes
Telescope: telescopio
Tennis: tenis

Tent: carpa
Tie up: abrochar
Tiger: tigre
Tired: cansado
Toboggan: tobogán
Today: hoy
Tomato: tomate
Too: también
Touch: tocar
Towel: toalla
Toy: juguete
Toy store: juguetería
Train: tren
Tulip: tulipán
Turtle: tortuga

U
Ugly Duckling: Patito Feo
Utensil: cubierto

V
Vacation: vacaciones
Vase: jarrón
Vet: veterinario
Video game: video
juego
Volleyball: vóleibol

W
Wait for: esperar a
Waltz: vals
Wash: lavar
Water: agua
Wedding gown:
vestido de novia
Weigh: pesar
Wildflower: flor silvestre
Winter: invierno
Witch: bruja
Wolf: lobo
Wooden paddles:
paletas de madera

Y
Year: año
Yellow: amarillo

Z
Zoo: zoológico

Diccionario alfabético

A
Abrazo: hug
Abrir: open
Abrochar: tie up
Abuela: grandma
Abuelo: grandpa
Acordeón: accordion
Acróbata: acrobat
Adorable: adorable
Aeropuerto: airport
Agua: water
Algodón de azúcar: cotton candy
Amarillo: yellow
Amigo: friend
Año: year
Ardilla: squirrel
Arena: sand
Autobús: bus
Atención: careful
Ayudar: help
Avión: plane
Azafata: hostess

B
Bádminton: badminton
Ballet: ballet
Banco: bank
Baño: bath
Barco: ship
Beso: kiss
Béisbol: baseball
Biberón: bottle
Bicicleta: bike
Blancanieves: Snow White
Bolsón: bag
Bonita: pretty
Botas: boots
Bruja: witch
Bucear: dive
Bueno: good

C
Cabra: goat
Caja: checkout counter
Calabaza: pumpkin
Calcetín: sock
Cama: bed
Camilla: examination table
Canción: song
Canicas: marbles
Cansado/a: tired
Cantar: sing
Caña de pescar: fishing rod
Caperucita Roja: Little Red Riding Hood
Caramelo: candy
Carpa: tent
Carro: car
Cartero: mailman
Casa: home
Castillo: castle
Celoso: jealous
Cena: dinner
Cenicienta: Cinderella
Cepillar: brush
Cereal: cereal
Cerdo: pig
Cesta: basket
Chupete: lollipop
Ciervo: deer
Cinco: five
Cinturón: seat belt
Circo: circus
Cita: appointment
Cocción: baking
Coche superrápido: super-fast car
Cocinar: cook
Cocodrilo: crocodile
Coleccionar: collect
Colonia: cologne
Columpio: swing
Comedero: feeder
Comer: eat
Comida: food
Compras: shopping
Concha: shell
Concierto: concert
Conejo: rabbit
Conejito: bunny
Contento: happy
Copa: glass
Cordero: lamb

Cosecha: harvest
Crecer: grow
Crema protectora: sunblock
Cuarto de baño: bathroom
Cubierto: utensil
Cuchara: spoon
Cuchillo: knife
Cuento: story
Cuerda: rope
Cumpleaños: birthday

D
Damas: checkers
Danzar: dance
Desayuno: breakfast
Desfile de modas: fashion show
Despegar: take off
Despertador: alarm clock
Dibujar: draw
Dictado: dictation
Dientes: teeth
Divertido: funny
Dormitorio: bedroom

E
Elefante: elephant
Elegir: choose
Encontrar: meet
Enfadado: mad
Escoba: broom
Escritorio: desk
Escuchar: listen
Espectáculo: show
Esperar: wait
Esqueleto: skeleton
Estetoscopio: stethoscope
Estrella: star
Estupenda: great

F
Facturar: check-in
Familia: family
Fantasma: ghost

Figura de acción: action toy
Flauta: flute
Flor silvestre: wildflower
Foca: seal
Fresa: strawberry
Fruta: fruit
Fútbol: soccer

G
Gansos: geese
Garaje: garage
Gaviota: seagull
Girasol: sunflower
Golf: golf
Gorila: gorilla
Gorro: hat
Gripe: flu
Guantes: gloves
Guitarra: guitar
Gustar: like

H
Hada: fairy
Hambriento: hungry
Hámster: hamster
Helado: ice cream
Hermana: sister
Hormiguero: anthill
Hoy: today

I
Impermeable: raincoat
Inflable: inflatable
Ingredientes: ingredients
Insecto: insect
Invierno: winter
Invitado: guest

J
Jardín: garden
Jarrón: vase
Juego: game
Jugar: play
Jugo: juice
Juguete: toy
Juguetería: toy store

L

Lamer: lick
Lápiz: pencil
Latido del corazón: heartbeat
Lavar: wash
Lavado: shampooing
Leche: milk
Lechuza: owl
León: lion
Libélula: dragonfly
Libro: book
Libro de recetas: cookbook
Limpiar: clean
Lirio: iris
Lista: list
Listo: ready
Llavero: key holder
Lobo: wolf
Loro: parrot
Luna: moon

M

Maestra/o: teacher
Mano: hand
Mantequilla: butter
Manzana: apple
Mantel: tablecloth
Mañana: morning
Mar: sea
Mariposa: butterfly
Mascota: mascot
Mechón de pelo: lock of hair
Médico: doctor
Medir: measure
Mercado: market
Merienda campestre: picnic
Mermelada: marmalade
Mezcla: batter
Monstruo: monster
Montaña rusa: roller coaster
Montar: ride
Museo: museum

N

Naranja: orange
Navidad: Christmas
Nevera: cooler
Nido: nest
Noche: night
Nombre: name

O

Obra de arte: masterpiece
Ojo: eye
Oler: smell
Otoño: fall

P

Padres: parents
Paletas de madera: wooden paddles:
Palomitas: popcorn
Pan: bread
Panecillo: muffin
Papa: potato
Papá Noel: Santa Claus
Parque: park
Parque de diversiones: amusement park
Parte: part
Pasar la fregona: mop
Pastel: pie
Patinar sobre el hielo: ice-skating
Pato: duck
Patito Feo: Ugly Duckling
Payaso: clown
Pecera: fish tank
Pegar: glue
Peine: comb
Pelícano: pelican
Pelo: hair
Peluche: fluffy toy
Peluquero: hairdresser
Pequeño: little
Pesar: weigh
Pescadería: fish section
Peter Pan: Peter Pan
Pez: fish
Piano: piano

Pie: foot
Pintar: paint
Pista: runway
Pizarra: blackboard
Plato: dish
Postre: dessert
Preferido: favorite
Primavera: spring
Primo: cousin
Princesa: princess
Probar: taste
Puerro: leek
Puesta de sol: sunset

Q

¡Qué bien luce!: Looks good!

R

Ramo: bouquet
Rápido: fast
Recién nacido: newborn baby
Recortar: cut out
Recreo: recess
Regalo: present
Ricitos de Oro: Goldilocks
Rojo: red
Rueda gigante: Ferris wheel

S

Sacar el polvo: dust
Salón: living room
Saltamontes: grasshopper
Salud: health
Saturno: Saturn
Saxo: sax
Secar: dry
Sol: sun
Sudadera: sweatshirt

T

También: too
Tarjeta: card
Telescopio: telescope

Tejón: badger
Tenedor: fork
Tenis: tennis
Tía: aunt
Tienda de animales: pet shop
Tigre: tiger
Tijeras: scissors
Toalla: towel
Tobogán: toboggan
Tocar: touch
Tomate: tomato
Tormenta: storm
Torta: cake
Tortuga: turtle
Tren: train
Triste: sad
Tronco flotante: floating tree trunk
Tulipán: tulip

U

Uña: nail

V

Vaca: cow
Vacaciones: vacation
Vals: waltz
Vaso: glass
Vela: candle
Vender: sell
Venir: come
Ventilar: air
Ver: see
Verano: summer
Vestido de novia: wedding gown
Vestirse: get dressed
Veterinario: vet
Video juego: video game
Vóleibol: volleyball

Z

Zanahoria: carrot
Zapatos: shoes
Zoológico: zoo
Zorro: fox

My First English/Spanish
Dictionary of Sentences

Author: Armelle Modéré
Illustrations: Armelle Modéré

First edition for the United States and Canada
(exclusively) and rest of the world (non-exclusively)
published in 2007 by Barron's Educational Series, Inc.
© Copyright 2007 by Gemser Publications, S.L.
El Castell, 38; 08329 Teià (Barcelona, Spain)

All inquiries should be addressed to:
Barron's Educational Series, Inc.
250 Wireless Boulevard
Hauppauge, NY 11788
http://www.barronseduc.com

ISBN-13: 978-0-7641-3865-2
ISBN-10: 0-7641-3865-0
Library of Congress Control Number 2007921751

Printed in China
9 8 7 6 5 4 3 2 1